Around Pattingham and Wombourne

IN OLD PHOTOGRAPHS

Around Pattingham and Wombourne

IN OLD PHOTOGRAPHS

Collected by MAY GRIFFITHS,
PETER LEIGH *and* MARY MILLS

Alan Sutton Publishing Limited
Phoenix Mill · Far Thrupp
Stroud · Gloucestershire

First published 1992

Copyright © May Griffiths, Peter Leigh and
Mary Mills 1992

Front cover illustration: A brake full of
day-trippers outside the Seven Stars in Seisdon
in the early part of the twentieth century. At this
time there were inns and teashops throughout
the area catering for tourists.

British Library Cataloguing
in Publication Data

Griffiths, May
Around Pattingham and Wombourne
in Old Photographs
I. Title
942.46

ISBN 0-86299-905-7

Typeset in 9/10 Sabon.
Typesetting and origination by
Alan Sutton Publishing Limited.
Printed in Great Britain by
WBC Print Limited, Bridgend.

Contents

Introduction

As can be seen from the map (p. 2), the area covered in this collection of photographs includes far more than the villages of Pattingham and Wombourne, extending to the parishes of Trysull and Seisdon, Patshull, Swindon and Himley. Lying in the south of the county of Staffordshire, these parishes are bounded by Shropshire to the west, the Black Country to the south-east and Wolverhampton to the east. Situated between an industrial conurbation and a sparsely inhabited area, they have acquired a common identity over the years based on serving the various needs of their industrialized neighbours. The region has been able to provide raw materials, food, manufactured articles and leisure facilities for the towns of the West Midlands.

The River Smestow and its tributaries run through the parishes, and its wide valley has a light, sandy soil that has proved ideal for the development of agriculture and market gardening. The Staffordshire and Worcestershire Canal follows the valley of the Smestow and runs through three of the parishes. Dramatic sandstone ridges outcrop throughout the region and buildings constructed of sandstone are a notable feature. Sand has been, and still is, quarried at various locations. This is suitable both for casting metals and for brick-making, and has been widely used in iron-making and other local industries. Gravel is also quarried in the area. In the days when metalworking depended on water power and was scattered in cottages and small workshops, the villages of south Staffordshire provided products such as nails and sheet metals for the larger towns and their factories.

During the nineteenth century when the towns of the West Midlands merged to become a conurbation, people began to look to the surrounding countryside for relief from the smoke and grime generated by industry. As can be seen in many of the photographs, not only did this area provide attractive scenery, dramatic woodland and large country houses, but also the villages were quick to furnish necessities, such as refreshments for the tourists and resting places for the horses that conveyed them through the area. In more recent times, while continuing to serve the leisure needs of nearby towns, the villages have all expanded to provide housing for people who work in the conurbation.

As well as having these geographical and economic ties, the different villages, with the exception of Patshull, have been linked politically since the formation of the Seisdon Poor Law Union in 1836. From 1894 until 1974 all of the parishes were in Seisdon Rural District. In 1992 they are all in the district of South Staffordshire.

The village of Pattingham is an ancient settlement dating back to Celtic times; a gold torque from this era was found there in 1700. Pattingham is sited on top of a sandstone ridge which drops down to the Smestow valley at the Clive to the south of the village. There have long been close links between Patshull and Pattingham, although they were until recently separate parishes, and the Astleys, who were lords of the manor of Patshull from 1451, acquired the lordship of Pattingham in 1725. The Astley family began to build the present Patshull Hall in the 1730s. The landscaping of the park caused many houses to be demolished, although it is not clear if there was ever a village at Patshull. The Astleys sold Patshull Hall to Sir George Pigot in 1765, along with land at Pattingham, and the Pigots in turn sold out to William Legge, the 4th Earl of Dartmouth, in 1848. The Dartmouths had lived in Sandwell Hall, West Bromwich, until mining operations at the Sandwell Colliery came uncomfortably close. Viscount Lewisham, later the 5th Earl, made improvements to the estate and built cottages for his workers that can still be seen all over the two parishes.

In the nineteenth century, Pattingham was a notorious haunt of men from the Black Country who came to watch bloodsports in the open space in front of the Pigot Arms. Day trippers also came to the village, especially when the many damson trees were in bloom: the village was nicknamed the 'Damson Village'. The damsons were grown for the vegetable dye that could be obtained from them and which was used to dye paper for packaging sugar. The population more than doubled in the 1950s when the building of new housing estates began and many of the older buildings, recorded in this book, were lost.

Although part of Wombourne ecclesiastical parish until 1888, Trysull has been a civil parish since the seventeenth century comprising the townships of Trysull and Seisdon. In 1900, Woodford Grange, which had been monastic land and not in a parish, became part of Trysull. The earliest mention of the parish occurs in the Domesday Book which recorded three settlements: Trysull, Seisdon and Cocortone. The latter was probably near to the present Beeches Farm and gave rise to the name Crockington (formerly Cockerton). The two manors of Trysull and Seisdon were joined together in 1557 and in 1633 were bought by Sir Hugh Wrottesley. They remained part of the Wrottesley Estate until 1929.

The area has always been agricultural. In 1914 the farms in the region were producing cereal crops, potatoes, pigs and poultry for the Black Country market. One local farmer was noted for the sucking pigs that he sold at 'wonderful prices' to Black Country colliers. Market gardening began in the mid-nineteenth century. Seisdon gave its name to the Hundred and later to the local government area. The village has always looked to Trysull for church and school, although there is evidence that Seisdon may have had a chapel in the twelfth century. Both villages catered for day trippers in Victorian and later times. In more recent years they have grown, although there has been more post-war housing constructed in Seisdon than Trysull.

Wombourne is an ancient parish that originally included Orton and Swindon. Swindon became a separate parish in 1896. The population was recorded as twenty-six working men at the time of the Domesday survey. Until the fourteenth century the manor of Wombourne was held by the Orton family with the manors of Orton, Swindon and Oxley. By the seventeenth century it had passed to the Wrottesleys. The land they still held in 1929 was sold when the estate was split up.

During the nineteenth century the population rose steadily, chiefly due to the number of people involved in nail-making. After 1861, when that trade declined, the village grew smaller. Between the wars, housing was built to the north of the village centre and the population has grown steadily since. Around 1930, when the Seisdon Rural District Council offices were moved from Trysull to Wombourne, it became an administrative centre for the region. It gained magistrates courts in 1968 and a civic centre in 1977, although the District Council offices were built at Codsall. From the 1950s, industrial estates have been established at Ounsdale and on the Bridgnorth Road, and the ten years between 1951 and 1961 saw a massive building programme. The Staffordshire and Worcestershire Canal passes through Wombourne, as did the Wolverhampton to Kingswinford railway which was opened in 1925 but had only a short life. The old railway line is now a linear park and the station houses a visitors' centre. There is a picnic area at the Bratch on the bank of the canal.

Swindon does not appear in the Domesday survey but may have been part of Himley at that time. It later formed the southern part of Wombourne Parish. The bridge over the Smestow in the centre of the village existed in 1435. Early ironworks were common in this part of Staffordshire and a forge was working on the Smestow Brook by the seventeenth century. This was probably the forge owned by a Mr Lidiat in 1636 which caused the loss of seven houses and other buildings when sparks set them alight. Ironworking continued in Swindon until 1976, when the British Steel Company closed the works that had originally been developed by E.P. and W. Baldwin. During the nineteenth century the population grew with people engaged in ironworking and nailing. There was also employment in agriculture in which vegetables and fruit trees were the most important crops. Swindon has expanded during the twentieth century, particularly since the Second World War. Modern housing estates have been built, including one on the site of the former steelworks at Swin Forge Way. The present village is very different from that recorded by the photographs in this book.

The parish of Himley lies on the border with Gornal in the Black Country and the industrialization of that area encroached into Himley Parish in the nineteenth and twentieth centuries. Himley and Swindon manors were held by the Dudley family from the fourteenth century. In 1947, William Humble Eric Ward, Earl of Dudley, sold his Himley Estate which also included land in the Wombourne and Swindon parishes. During his lordship the area was exploited for its coal: Baggeridge colliery, opened in 1912, was the last major coal mine to operate in the South Staffordshire coalfield. Baggeridge Wood, which lies across the border between Himley and Wombourne, was a major tourist attraction in the first half of the twentieth century, but was reduced in size when many of the trees were felled during the Second World War. Baggeridge Country Park now covers the site of the colliery and part of the wood.

The collection of photographs included in this book both records the changes that this area has undergone and reflects the nature of a region that, although still predominantly rural, has been affected in many ways by its proximity to a major industrial conurbation. The captions for each section have been prepared by whoever knows it best: in the case of Pattingham, Peter Leigh; Wombourne, May Griffiths; and Trysull and Seisdon and Swindon, Himley and Baggeridge, Mary Mills.

Pattingham

Newgate, now renamed Wolverhampton Road, *c.* 1908. This rural scene had barely changed in 200 years before the 1950s. The view from the crossroads along Wolverhampton Road is very different today. Unfortunately not one of the buildings seen here remains. The Pound in the foreground was near the School Drive, and thatched Hollybush Cottage was near the present entrance to Newgate, the name retained by the 1960s development off Wolverhampton Road. The lighter, timber-framed seventeenth-century cottages (demolished in 1938) were in front of the modern bungalows, and the darker cottages were in front of Martin Thomas' shop. In the 1920s and '30s Pattingham was a popular wagonette outing for the townsfolk of Wolverhampton and the Black Country.

Procession of the Independent Order of Oddfellows, Manchester Unity Friendly Society. Here the Loyal Victoria Lodge (Pattingham) is leaving Highgate House in Wolverhampton Road on Whit Monday. Before the Second World War, most people in the village belonged to this society, children being enrolled from the age of twelve.

The Cottage, built in 1851 in Dartmouth Estate style, was situated next to the present-day doctor's surgery in Wolverhampton Road and was demolished in 1971 when Newgate was extended.

Wolverhampton Road. The trees are where the entrance to Orchard Close is today, which was the site of the original Free School built in 1702. Ivy House (to the right of the trees) was the first post office in 1844. Note the tall chimney from the bread ovens in Bramall's Bakery adjoining the cottages. This bakehouse was demolished when the cottages were renovated prior to the orchard being developed for a bungalow (no. 30) and a house (no. 32). The Bramall's stopped baking in the 1920s.

Wolverhampton Road, 1922. This view is from almost the same position as above, showing the wall and entrance to Yew Tree House (now Merchant Close), Hollybush Cottage (now the entrance to Newgate) and the Poors Trust Cottages (left foreground). The original Yew Tree House was in Regency style, with iron railings similar to Ivy House, and was located in front of the present building.

The Poors Trust Cottages, *c.* 1902. On the left, adjacent to the present school drive in Wolverhampton Road, were the Poors Trust Cottages. There were three cottages at the front and two back-to-back. They were all demolished *c.* 1961. The income from rents was distributed annually on Easter Monday and at Christmas for the benefit of the poor in the parish.

The Parish Reading Room, *c.* 1902. Above the doorway behind the man on the right is a sign for the Reading Room. This came into use in 1886 when the Earl of Dartmouth offered the use of the upstairs club room of the then disused Roebuck Inn, for a nominal rent of 1*s.* per annum, for the use of the working men of Pattingham. The public weigh-bridge can be seen in the roadway outside the first doorway. The Pound, on the left, was demolished *c.* 1966.

Buck Corner, *c.* 1920s. This was formerly the Roebuck Inn (1834–85). In 1927 the magnificent chimney fell through the roof – the repair is still noticeable today. In the 1930s, Dr Legge held his surgery here on Tuesdays and Fridays. The meadow opposite (next to the Pound) was where the travelling fair was held each Whit Monday.

The Poplars, *c.* 1906. This building probably dates from the first quarter of the nineteenth century and has fine views overlooking the playing fields. The Poplars was the post office from 1884 to 1907. The post office signs can be seen over the bottom right window.

Pattingham House, 1950s. The house was built in 1753 by architect Wm. Baker of Audlem, who had previously been engaged on work at Patshull Hall. It has had a chequered history. In the mid-nineteenth century it was a boarding school for young ladies. The adjacent Jockey Cottages (the white buildings in the centre) acquired their name when Mr Bullock ran horse-racing stables in the 1930s from Pattingham House. Later, greyhounds were trained there, before it became a private nursing home (maternity) and then a private residence. Granny Caddick's sweet shop was called Meadow View (built in 1692) and the post office next door was called Church View. These cottages were demolished to make way for an unsympathetic shopping development.

The Pigot Arms, *c.* 1908.

Coronation Day, 1953. St Chad's Cottage, in the background, was the village newsagent. Customers were trusted to serve themselves, put the money on the green saucer on the table and take the correct change.

The Pigot Arms, c. 1920. This most famous landmark of Pattingham is thought to have started its life in the mid-eighteenth century as The London Prentice. It could have been built on the site of the New Inn which dated from the early 1600s. In the 1820s it was known as the Kings Arms, but from the mid-1830s its name has stayed as a constant reminder of the Pigot family who owned Patshull Estate which included much of the land in Pattingham.

The Albrighton Hunt meeting in the Bull Ring, *c.* 1923. In the early nineteenth century, Pattingham was noted as a place for old English sports such as bull baiting, badger baiting, and dog and cock fighting, the two latter being favourite Sunday sports. The area between the Pigot Arms, the church and the village hall is generally described as the Bull Ring.

Harold Taylor, 1936. The butchers shop was sited in the Pigot Arms. This was the retail outlet for Peter Oliver at Meadleys Farm who had started his own abattoir.

The Pigot Arms, *c.* 1944. During the Second World War the Pigot Arms was the HQ of 'D' Company Home Guard.

Postmen outside the post office, *c.* 1928. Left to right: Jim Trace, Tom Richards, Harold Kirkham, Millie Bowen, Alice Jones, Alfred Price.

High Street, *c.* 1902. This scene has changed little. Beyond the Pigot Arms on the left is the adjoining seventeenth-century cottage (now disappeared) which used to be connected to St Chad's Cottage. On the opposite side of the road is Pattingham Stores which is thought to be the site of the Great Fire of 10 September 1678. Several houses, workshops, barns and outhouses were burned down, together with much of the church. This grocery store (Lychgate House) became the post office after Ivy House and before The Poplars.

School outing, *c.* 1947.

Whit Monday gathering of the Oddfellows Friendly Society. The staffs are held by officers of the society, often topped by a bunch of 'whitsuntide boss' – the flowers of the viburnum snowball bush which was as common as the damson trees in the gardens in Pattingham.

High Street, 1920. Apart from the loss of the cottages next to Price's Smithy (in the middle distance), this scene has changed very little. On the left is St Chad's Cottage containing the adjoining Harper's Smithy, with the Crown Beerhouse beyond. The cottages have been converted to form Chad House (this was when the light-coloured cottages disappeared). The trees, hedges and sandstone walls have now made way for Old Smithy Close, but in contrast to what has happened to the eastern side of the village, developments have been implemented sympathetically. The clock in the end of St Chad's Cottage is thought to be the original church clock, salvaged from the time when the steeple was added in 1871 by the 5th Earl of Dartmouth in memory of his father. James Harper was the sexton and Captain of the Tower at the time, and lived at St Chad's Cottage.

The Celebration (outside the bakehouse), *c.* 1918. The reason for the celebration is not clear, but it seems likely that it was a welcome home for soldiers returning from the First World War.

View of the bakehouse from the church tower, July 1924. The bakehouse is in the High Street situated between the old Pattingham Stores and the Dartmouth-style Chergordon (formerly Beausale). It was sympathetically converted to a private residence in 1979. During 1941–3, Catholic church services for evacuees from Liverpool were held in the room over the bakehouse.

Harvest Supper in the bakehouse, *c.* 1948. Left to right: Mrs Monkton, Doris Pugh, Jessie Low, Vera Gittins, Mary Lycett, Milly Gittins, Nancy Caddick, Revd Prime, Graham Bull, Mr Inett, Joe Caddick.

Miller's stores and bakery, *c.* 1922. Note the steps up to the cottages (now Chad House).

Coal cart from College Farm outside Price's Smithy, *c.* 1920. Left to right: Joe Law, Fred Bacchus, Alfred Price.

The Price family in the yard at the back of the smithy, *c.* 1910. John Price arrived from Hereford in 1840 as an apprentice blacksmith and eventually took over the smithy. Left to right: Tom, Alfred, Mary, Bill, -?-, Tom Snr, -?-.

Mrs Russell outside Rock Cottage in High Street. (Mr Russell was the village cobbler.) The cottage is built from locally made bricks which are smaller than modern ones. The brickworks were situated in Nurton Hill Road and at Rudge.

Bay Cottage, situated behind 16 High Street and accessed by the alley at the side. Opposite the cottage was a shed where George Price repaired bicycles during the 1920s and '30s.

Pattingham Hall. This house dated partly from the seventeenth century, but had a timber-framed wing added in 1935, constructed from old materials. It was located on the corner of High Street and Hall End Lane and was demolished in 1968.

West End towards the Hall, 1902. The cottages in the foreground were occupied by the Bateman family from 1929 to 1934. The one at the end was converted into a fish and chip shop. Beyond lies Jasmine House which still exists today. For the latter half of the nineteenth century, the timbered building was owned by the Stanford family who were horse and fruit dealers. In the 1930s the adjoining potato warehouse became Mr Fox's butchers shop. In the background, Alston still had its original Regency windows.

The Working Men's Club in 1920. This club existed in 1896 and was part of Pear Tree Yard, named after the Tettenhall Dick pear trees. Behind the club were three or four small terraced cottages. At the back of the yard were cottages, lavatories and pigsties. At the front of the yard farther along the High Street were two other cottages (Granny Caddick's and her shop that sold pop and cigarettes), a double-gated entrance to the yard, gents toilets for the club and a warehouse. The fourth side of the yard was a brick wall. In the centre of the yard was a large pear tree, with other pear trees against the brick wall.

The new Working Men's Club was built in 1957 by Bradford Bros., on the original site of Pear Tree Yard in the High Street.

Marlbrook Lane, *c.* 1910. During the 1930s, George Bowker lived at Marlbrook Cottage. He did carpentry, hedge-cutting and pig-killing. Most people in Pattingham kept a pig or two and George occasionally performed the service at home, but mostly at customers' premises.

West End towards Rudge Road, *c.* 1908. The Primitive Methodist Chapel operated from 1868 to 1884. In 1894 it was sold and converted to a house, and subsequently became the village stores and post office. In the distance is the police house. The cell was situated on the Rudge Road side and comprised a toilet, wooden bed and round, wooden pillow. The police station was later replaced (*c.* 1960) by one in Wolverhampton Road, next to Highgate House, but this was closed *c.* 1974.

Pattingham Church exterior. This picture was taken by Bennett Clark, a noted Wolverhampton photographer of Edwardian times.

Marlbrook Cottage, *c.* 1903. Left to right: Emily Titley, Mrs Humphriston. Note the washing out to dry on the hedge!

Bill Poynton, sexton during the 1920s and '30s, was accomplished on the church carillion, which he played most evenings. He was fond of giving a rendition for the benefit of visitors to the village. Bill was noted for ensuring the church clock kept perfect time and lived in the Poors Trust Cottages in Wolverhampton Road. The chimes of the church clock were restored in 1935 in memory of Mr Poynton, who was ringer for 50 years, sexton for 22 years and chorister for 65 years.

The vicarage (according to the *Victoria County History*) is of the late eighteenth century, with an extension (Glebe House) added in 1863. Planning permission has been granted to demolish this extension to enable another house to be built. The most famous occupant was Revd William George Greenstreet. He arrived as curate in 1843, became the vicar in 1847 and remained until his death in 1900 – a total of fifty-seven years service. The son of a general, he was born in Madras, India, but came to England to be educated. He graduated from Christ's College, Cambridge. Throughout the Victorian era he was without doubt the most influential person in Pattingham, initiating many reforms. The vicarage became a private residence in 1990.

Norman Bramall demonstrates the carillion, February 1968. Made mostly of wood, the carillion is like a large musical box with steel pegs set in a wooden drum. A weight drives the drum at a speed controlled by a set of wheels and an air brake, while the pegs lift levers connected to hammers and so play a tune on a set of bells. There are eight bells which weigh approximately 57 cwt in total.

Bellringers for the Victory Peel, 1945. Left to right: Charlie Ray, Albert Monkton, Arthur Johnson, Jim Ray, Tom Ray, Harold Ray, Harold Warner, Len Handy.

Pattingham Church interior, *c.* 1920s. This picture was also Bennett Clark's work. The ornate chandelier in the foreground was probably one of several such candle-holders that illuminated the church once. The present chandelier is inscribed with the name of Pattingham Church. It was returned *c.* 1982 by a lady in the South of England, into whose possession it had fallen. It now hangs over the steps in the Lady Chapel. This view of the nave, chancel and sanctuary faces East. The pillars on the left belong to the Norman arch which is the oldest part of the building. The Reredos (in front of the two lancet windows) was donated by the Earl of Dartmouth in 1890 and is of Derbyshire alabaster. The carving is exquisite, and the height and size of this elaborate stone are considered to have added dignity to this otherwise plain early English chancel.

Members of the Red Cross outside the vicarage. Note the splendid Victorian porch which was replaced by a window in the early 1950s. Front row, left to right: Mrs Warner, Miss Nicholls, Mrs Harris, Renee Shanks, Mary Lycett, Jessie Inett, Mrs Boswell, Mrs Crutchley, Mrs Dyke, Mrs Wall, Mrs Matthews, Mrs Page.

Wedding group, December 1927. Such photographs were often taken in the photographer's studio. This one was for Mr and Mrs Bull of Dudleys in Dudley Street, Wolverhampton. Back row, left to right: Sam Kirby, Horace Bull, Alice Bull née Williams, Elsie Williams. Front row, left to right: Mary Jones, Mary Bull, Joseph Williams, Nora Bull, Alice Jones.

The golf clubhouse, Patshull, was loaned by Lord Dartmouth to the Home Guard during the Second World War for use as an Officers' Mess. The building is still in existence and is used by Scouts. The original nine-hole golf course has disappeared. The present Patshull Golf Course is a new development centred around the Temple on Patshull Pool.

No. 17 Platoon of the 24th Staffordshire (Tettenhall) Battalion, Home Guard. Their headquarters were in the Reading Room, Pattingham. Back row, left to right: Jack Collett, Bert Gittins, Frank Parker, Jack Pritchard, Alec Martin, Ted Pritchard, Jack Royall, George Wheeler, Alf Sparrow, Bill Bowker. Front row, left to right: Jim Burgess, Bill Head, Cyril Smith, Lt D.G. Hann, Harold Taylor, Sid Jones, Jack French.

D Company Home Guard Spigot Mortar Team at Patshull, *c.* 1943. Left to right: Pte S. Weston, Pte J.R. Pinches, L/Cpl. G.A. Stokes, L/Cpl. A.J. Chamberlain, Sgt J.T. Ray.

D Company Northover Projectors Team, *c.* 1943. Left to right: Pte K.R. Caseley, Pte T.A. Postance, Sgt S.T. Ray, Pte H.T. Downes, Pte H. Parkes.

The school, Westbeech Road. The National School opened in 1875 on a site donated by Lord Dartmouth who also met the building costs above the amount raised by public subscription. There were three schoolrooms, one each for boys, girls and infants, and two classrooms. The trees make a dramatic difference to a scene that otherwise has changed little. Perhaps there is a lesson to be learned that when the trees have to be removed for safety reasons, there should not be a fifty-year delay before replacing them.

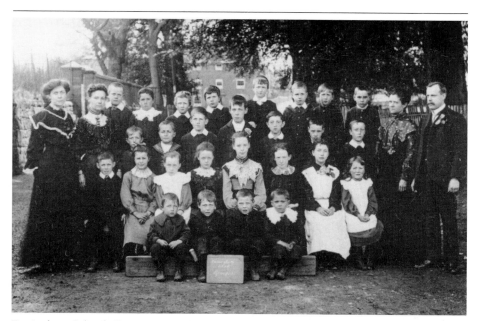

Pattingham School, Group 1, *c*. 1906.

The playing field, *c*. 1908. The fence around the field was augmented by a hedge along Westbeech Road, which brings relief to the starkness of the bare railings which feature today.

Pasford Farm, 1951. This is part of the Crown Estate and is situated on the Patshull Road on the left before the entrance to the golf and fishing complex which is of part of the new Patshull Park Hotel. The house is in Dartmouth style and is in a beautiful setting overlooking the Worfe valley. The farm contains the cascade and eel trap that control the flow of water from Patshull Pool.

Pasford Mill, June 1951. There are references to a mill at Pasford as early as 1314. The present mill dates from the mid-nineteenth century. It continued in operation grinding animal feed until the early 1940s, when the bank of the mill stream collapsed during a flood.

The Park, Pasford Farm. Planting potatoes at the Park, Pasford Farm, April 1951. The horse is pulling trays of seed potatoes. Two women carried a tray and planted by hand. Left to right: Doug Lane, Bill Reynolds, -?-, -?-, -?-, Mrs Hughes, Mrs Bennett, Kath Ray, Kate Ray.

Pasford Farm, 1951. The machine is a Massey Harris 21 self-propelled combine with a 12 ft cut. Left to right: Ken Russell, Reg Harrison (driver), Charlie Stanford, -?-, Harrison Jnr.

Harvesting at Fox Inn on the Bridgnorth Road at Shipley, 1949. The Foster threshing machine is being driven by Charlie Law.

Law's threshing box from Buck Corner, c. 1895. Some years later, a spark from the fire set the threshing box alight and burned it out. The dogs in the picture were there to kill the rats. Left to right: George Law, Fred Russell, Mr Bowker, -?-, Francis Law, -?-, George Pritchard.

The farm ladies. Back row, left to right: Mrs Howell, Mrs Sargent, Mrs Jane Guest, Mrs Jennie Walker. Front row, left to right: Mrs Monkton, Mrs Monkton Snr., Martha Davies, Rosie Sargent, Mrs Sam Davies.

Logging in Patshull Park by the Parkes family, *c.* 1920. Timber was collected from as far afield as the Welsh border, on subcontract to John S. Hickman in Wolverhampton. Jim and Arthur Parkes and their families lived in a cottage in the cherry tree orchard, now part of Noverton in Nurton Hill Road.

Clive Farm, 1956. The famous Pattingham herd of British Friesians are coming in for milking. Tragedy overcame Clive Farm in 1940 when an outbreak of brucellosis mallentensis occurred, necessitating the slaughter of all livestock on the farm. A year later the Friesian herd was started from Elmwood Bulls. Skilled and careful breeding produced a herd which became famous for its high milk yield – several cows produced over 2,000 gallons of milk a year. The herd was sold *c.* 1967.

Straw bales at Clive Farm, 1953. There are over 6,000 bales in here. They were used for cattle bedding during the winter.

Bagging potatoes at Lower Barns, 1962. Left to right: Mrs Clark, Norman Williamson, George Williamson, Bert Gittins, Mrs Dixon.

Stooked wheat at Clive Farm, 1935.

The village hall, *c.* 1929. This building was opened by Lord and Lady Dartmouth on 15 December 1922. Lord Dartmouth donated the site and, by public subscription, a timber army hut was purchased, left over from the First World War. In 1925/6 it was increased in length by ten feet and a verandah was added. The tennis court was then added in 1929. Beyond the tennis court was a bowling green. Electric lighting was installed in 1931. The Trust Deed for the village hall stated that 'no wine, beer or spirits or other intoxicating liquors shall be sold on the said premises'. A new hall was built in 1966, but the old timber army hut from the First World War is still in use at Stanlow Farm (on the road to Ackleton).

Tennis match, *c.* 1929. The tennis court was not a great success because weeds and docks quickly grew on it.

Girls' Friendly Society, *c.* 1930s. Back row, left to right: Ivy Newby, Ruth Taylor, Nancy Law, Olive Johnson, Sally Noakes, Peggy Nock, Annie Ray. Front row, left to right: Gladys Inett, Doris Morgan, Joan Edwards.

Girls' Friendly Society, 1937. Back row, left to right: Ruth Taylor, Jim Nock, Isobel Lloyd, Peggy Nock, Sally Noakes, Annie Ray, Nancy Law, Doris Morgan, Gladys Inett, Olive Johnson, -?-, Ivy Newby, George Edwards. Middle row, left to right: -?-, Barbara Sargent, -?-, Kathy Ray, Dorothy Scriven, -?-, Vera Bacchus, -?-, Alwyn Evans, Browny Johnson, Jack Taylor. Front row, left to right: Lilly Johnson, Nellie Lloyd, Pru Lloyd, -?-, -?-, -?-, -?-, Barbara Taylor, Janet Edwards, Alice Brooks, Flossie French, Edna Monkton, Charlie Edwards.

Pattingham Bowling Club outside the village hall, 1927. The group includes: Albert Monkton, Stanley Nock, Fred Matthews, Victor Griffiths, Wilf Taylor, J. Ray, Harry Bramall, Albert Edwards, Jack Castello, John Edwards, Harold Taylor, Fred Scriven, Jack Speake, William Nock, Mr Crutchley, Charlie Holder, Albert Bentley, Lilly Ray, Alice Bramall, Amy Edwards, Harry Matthews, Leslie Brazier and Harold Ray.

The Auxilliary Fire Service in Pigot Garden, June 1941. Codsall firemen had been training with Pattingham Fire Service at Patshull Pool, with the trailer pump towed behind an old converted Chrysler car which was garaged at the Retreat. Meetings were held in the barn at the Retreat. Back row, left to right: Norman Harris, Len Handy, Harold Ray, Charlie Law, Bevill Bentley, Bill Smith, Stan Bentley, Tom Price, John Strong, Charlie Pritchard, Herbert Tooth, -?- (Codsall AFS). Middle row: all Codsall AFS except Jim Parkes (centre). Front row, left to right: Tony Taylor, Leslie Williamson, Clifford Rowley.

Pattingham football team, 1923. The football field was loaned by Myatts the brewers and was situated behind what is now the Pigot Arms car park, extending beyond the gardens of St Chad's Cottage and the Crown pub. Access was obtained by a path at the side of the old post office, probably where the Stars Shop is now.

Westbeech Road from the church tower, 1935. College Farm is in splendid isolation. In the foreground is the site of the present football pitch. The field on the left is Pool Meadow which at one time contained three large pools. The top centre of the picture is locally known as the Monument (after a stone pillar that used to be located in the grass triangle where Nurton Hill Road branches off to the right). A lodge (Dower House) to the Patshull Estate is on the left.

The post van and postmen. Left to right: Tom Bowen, Ted Richards, Alfred Price.

Clive Farm dairy van.

An Invicta steamroller parked in the meadow opposite Buck Corner, *c.* 1950. The regular driver was George Cox. The steamroller used to tow a caravan for use as a mess room for roadworkers (and occasionally for sleeping in overnight if they were some distance from home).

The no. 16 bus passing Hollybush Cottage in Wolverhampton Road.

The Elms. This building was auctioned in 1912, together with West View (an adjacent cottage with a barn and cowsheds). It is described as a Georgian residence with a carriage drive and two gates. The outbuildings comprised a dairy, coach and harness rooms, and several other outhouses, while the garden contained a vinery and greenhouse heated by hot water. The building was demolished in 1963 and the site is now occupied by nos. 55 to 65 Clive Road. Surprisingly, very few photographic records have survived of the buildings in Clive Road, particularly of the fine buildings like the Retreat and West House, both of which were owned by farmers in Victorian times.

The Clive Farmhouse, 1916. The house was built in 1875 following a fire in the original farmhouse which was on the other side of the road (see opposite).

The Clive Farm complex, 1957. On the right is the Clive Farmhouse, built in 1875. It became a private residence in 1987. The barns along the roadside (centre) have now disappeared. In the centre foreground is the site of the original thatched farmhouse. It was rebuilt as two cottages (below). The latest farmhouse, built in 1987, is located centre left. There has been a settlement recorded on this site since 1312.

Site of the original Clive Farm. These two cottages at the Clive arose from the ashes of the thatched farmhouse which burned down in 1874. The left-hand part was extended in 1987 by Roland Williamson, whose family farmed the Clive for fifty-five years.

Behind the Crown pub, c. 1940. Back row, left to right: Wilf Taylor, Harry Gregory, Horace ?, two visitors from Claverley, Jack French, Bill Ash, Sam Ray, Jim Burgess, Mrs Taylor. Front row, left to right: Harry Everall, Geoff Warrilow, Henry Parkes, Jack Ray, Tom Ray, Alec Martin.

Annual trip to the seaside, c. 1936. Back row, left to right: -?-, Mrs Shaw, Bessie Shaw, Lil Monkton, -?- (coach driver), Mrs Ray, Florrie French, Minnie Harley, May Newby, Mrs Kidson, Mrs Swaite, Sue Lloyd, Lil Tracey, Mrs Scriven, Mrs Russell, Mrs Morris, Mrs Hadley. Front row, left to right: Mrs Ashley, Mrs Humphries, Mrs Brazier, Mrs Bate, Mrs Sargent, Grace Sargent, Mrs Smith, John Scriven.

John Williamson unloading wheat at Lower Barns, 1935. There is aerial photographic evidence to indicate that a Romano-British settlement probably existed at Lower Barns.

The Fox Inn, Shipley, c. 1908. This is an old coaching stage and famous hostelry on the Bridgnorth Road.

Entrance to Patshull Hall, Patshull *c.* 1902. Patshull Hall was built *c.* 1740 by Sir John Astley, who sold it to the Pigot family in 1765. This gateway is thought to have been added by George Pigot in 1820.

Patshull Hall from the south-west, *c.* 1908. The 1st Baronet, Sir George Pigot (governor of Madras for about ten years), died in 1771. His title devolved to his brother, Lt-Gen. Sir Robert Pigot, the 2nd Baronet, who also inherited the celebrated Pigot diamond. He was an officer of high reputation during the Great American War, and was so distinguished at Bunker's Hill that he obtained his colonelcy of the 38th Regiment of Foot. Sir Robert Pigot, the 4th Baronet (MP for Bridgnorth), sold the property to Lord Dartmouth in 1848. Capability Brown was employed to do the landscaping of the park, and this involved changing the size and shape of Patshull Pool to that which exists today.

The kitchen, Patshull Hall.

Wolverhampton Naturalist and Archaeological Society excursion to Patshull Park, 18 June 1904. 'Arriving at Patshull the party were [sic] conducted through the vineries, peach houses, gardens etc, for which Patshull is so justly famed.'

The Bridge, Patshull Pool, c. 1908. Fishing at Patshull has never been more popular than today. It has brought acclaim and visitors from far and wide to enjoy the sport of fly fishing for trout at Patshull Fishery. The ancient hamlet of Hardwick does not lie submerged under the pool, which was once supposed, but was sited in the park field which runs along Patshull Road and meets the end of the spur of the pool which faces the modern Patshull Park Hotel.

The Duke and Duchess of York arrive at Patshull Hall, 23 July 1900. Royalty were frequent visitors to the hall throughout the Dartmouth period. The hall now lies empty and its future is uncertain. Let us hope that this fine building can be usefully employed and restored to its former glory.

SECTION TWO
Wombourne

Wombourne Wodehouse (pronounced Woodhouse) from the south, *c.* 1950. Records sug-
gest there has been a home here for almost 800 years. The story began in the mid-twelfth
century when William le Coq (anglicized to Cook) asked the Baron of Dudley for a clear-
ing in the forest of Kinver above the brook on the eastern edge of the manor of
Wombourne. His request was granted at a rent of 12*d.* a year. His descendants, 'the people who lived at the house in the wood', evolved their surname from that description and
by the fourteenth century were well known as the Woodhouse family. They occupied the
house and land for nearly five centuries, during which time they played a prominent part
in village affairs. In 1708 the property passed to the Helliers, later to the Shaw Helliers,
and in 1981 to John and Carolyn Phillips. In its long history the house has never been
sold. Over the centuries there have been many alterations and additions to the house
(there was a plan in 1803 to pull it down and build a neo-classical villa), but the core is
still the late medieval timber-framed hall-house dated about 1350. The Wodehouse is a
welcoming home in pleasant gardens alongside the Wom Brook, enjoyed not only by the
owners, but by the thousands of visitors with whom they share it on behalf of local and
national causes and charities.

St Benedict Biscop Church interior, 1910. This is now twice the size of the medieval building of which the tower, spire and part of the west and north-west walls survive. Founded in 910, it is unique in England as the only ancient parish church dedicated to the seventh-century Northumbrian bishop Benedict, founder of Monkwearmouth and Jarrow Abbeys.

St Benedict Biscop Choir, 1930s. Back row, left to right: Clem Sadler, Leslie Key, Albert Piper, Harry Key, William Jones, Harry England, -?-, Lesley Taylor, -?-, Rupert Lloyd (organist), Tom Jones (churchwarden). Front row, left to right: Ken Stevens, Len Guest (still in the choir), Sam Holder, George Rowlands, Jack Guest, Bill Marson, Gordon Guest, Alan Moore, Bert Marson, Rob Cooke, Ernest Guest, Gerald Sadler, Desmond Guest, George Cartright. The cross bearer is Hal Langley, the vicar's youngest son.

The old Arbour Tree, 1920. Dead or not, many villagers would not part with it, but arguments were silenced when one dark night 'person or persons unknown' set fire to it. Another was put in its place, for it marked a special meeting place since the village began. The present Arbour Tree is in the path opposite the church gate.

High Street, 1930s. Even though there was a for-and-against war of words over it, the high wall around the cricket field was taken down in the late 1950s. The Small Brook is now piped under the path. In those days, a branch of it went down Mill Lane, and another in front of the shops to the delight of children who splashed in it, shoes and all. The fence in front of the house (the chapel manse) has gone. These premises are now a shop and offices.

Outside the Vine, *c.* 1898. On the left is Waverley Farm and beyond it two cottages (one of which was a shop), now the police station and houses. The Small Brook ran along the road edge and often, after a storm, into the houses as well. The Vine is on the right, and the building in its yard became Wombourne's first factory when Joe Timms from Sedgley set up his safe works there in 1926.

The Bush public house, or the Old Bush as it was when William Jones was the licensee in the late nineteenth century. There was a secluded garden behind with wooden benches and tables, as good a place as any to while away a summer evening. The present pub stands on the same site in what is now High Street, formerly Over Street.

Small Brook, *c.* 1950. It is also known as Townsend and Sodom. 'Small Brook' from the tiny stream from Orton Hills, now piped underground from the willow trees in the picture; 'Townsend' from the edge of the early village crofts, beyond which were the open fields; and 'Sodom', which is anybody's guess! The houses above were demolished in the 1970s for road widening and for the present bungalows and flatlets of Waterfield House.

Red Lion Hill, 1920s. Once on the A449, this was bypassed in the 1960s by a new section cut out of the Birch Hill behind the pub. On the right is the police station and sergeant's home (where the car is standing). Just below in the nineteenth century was the Victoria Inn. The area and the brook bridge nearby is called Rushford, and was so called before the fourteenth century.

A bird's eye view, 1967. There have been many changes since. The council offices (square complex, above) are now the civic centre; slightly below are the old maltings which are now flatlets for the elderly; on the right of the church are the vicarage gardens which are now Manor Court and Vicarage Close; almost opposite to the right is now the police sta-

tion complex; at the end of the same road, Waterfield House has replaced Small Brook Cottages. The more one looks the more there is to find. God's acre behind the church is almost full.

In the Bull Ring, an ancient name denoting the place where the cruel sport of bull baiting with dogs took place. Barclays Bank is on the site of what was once a nail factor's house with a warehouse attached. When the hand-made nail trade flourished in the mid-nineteenth century, there were three such premises where iron rods were collected and nails returned a week later. Whole families of all ages made nails at home in awful conditions. It was rightly called 'a sweated trade'.

This is opposite the above site and the house still exists as Grove Cottage. In the nineteenth century it was the home of the constable and later of the district nurse. Netley House, just visible on the left, was home to a maltster in the eighteenth century. The maltings were behind and preceded the later ones in Walk Lane. Wombourne's first automatic telephone exchange occupied the space on the right of the cottage in the 1930s. After 1953 it had other uses, including a jeweller's premises, and was demolished in 1991 for an access road to new dwellings behind.

The constable's house was at the top of Planks Lane in the 1930s and '40s, and the cell was at the back. The above premises were sold before the new police station in School Road in 1947 was ready, so for some time prisoners were taken to Divisional Headquarters at Willenhall. As one officer put it, 'it was a long way to lug a drunk, so perhaps that is why most of them were sent home'.

Windmill Bank, late 1930s. Parade days are proud days and worth remembering. Coming down The Bank was easier than going up. A long time ago it was 'the way to the wind-mill' situated on the present New Inns site. The sails last turned long before 1800. The nineteenth-century mill was near to the present Waverley Gardens. Note the old houses half demolished and the present Boxley's butchers shop on the left.

Windmill Bank, late 1920s. This view is from half-way down The Bank looking towards cottages and farm buildings at the top of the present Maypole Street. The houses were close together all down the east side as far as the junction with Church Road and half-way down on the other. In the foreground are little Jack Mansell and Mr George Tongue.

Station Road. Before the Great Western Railway made its mark on Wombourne the whole length of the way from Windmill Bank to the canal locks was Bratch Lane. In May 1925, when the line opened, the residents who had waited the best part of forty years since the first plans celebrated by renaming a portion of it Station Road. On the right are the village's first council houses built in the mid-1930s. On the left is the end of a row of four houses called Jackson's Building, which were at the corner of Mount Road and Station Road. These were demolished after the Second World War.

Bratch Station, Wombourne, c. 1929. A railway was planned in 1865 from Wolverhampton to Bridgnorth through Trysull, with a branch southwards from Wombourne. However, only the branch was completed and that not until 1925. After only seven years it was closed to passenger traffic, but went on as a busy and successful goods line until 1968. The track's future lay as part of a long-distance footpath.

The men who built the railway. These hard-working navvies had no idea as they sweated making cuttings and embankments, laying track and building stations that in less than half a century another set of workmen would be making their iron way into a footway. Nevertheless, as the Kingswinford Branch Railway Walk, it is proving as much an asset to Wombourne and South Staffordshire as did the railway in its short life.

The Planks Lane depot of the railway contractors, Perry and Company, in 1913/14. The view is southwards towards Common Road Bridge. The tall trees (middle left) show the line of the Wom Brook and, apart from a few acres close to it, all the rest of the fields shown are now built over.

The last passenger train called on 13 June 1964. Although primarily for goods from 1932, the line was used for occasional excursions (see p. 67). In 1937 when the Royal Show was held in Wrottesley Park, it was invaluable for transporting materials and livestock to Tettenhall, with just a short road journey to the showground. Surely its finest hour was after the D-Day allied landings in Normandy when the wounded were flown back to England and dispersed by rail to hospitals all over the country. The Bratch, because of its isolation and its passing loop, was ideal for these trains. About forty came, usually after darkness, to waiting ambulances and volunteers alerted from all over South Staffordshire, ready to take the men to hospitals in Wolverhampton and others in the region. Less secret trains brought the men in hospital blue to convalesce at Himley Hall.

The school outing, 1930s. Since at this time most children spent the summer holidays at home, the school outing was a red letter day. John Apse hired a train (the middle coach was the bar) and transported practically all Wombourne for a magic day at the seaside. They left Bratch just after dawn on the second Saturday in July and got back just after dawn on Sunday. They were unforgettable days, always recalled with a smile. Left to right: Hilda Hayward, Agnes Gregory, -?-, -?-, Doris Haynes, -?-. For these girls it was a case of a pretty dress and knickers worth showing, and their cares disappearing with the ebbing tide.

The same school outing. Left to right: Mrs Marsden, Rose Wood, Ernest Guest, Harold Marsden, -?-, George Marsden, -?-, -?-, Mrs Pace, Mrs Pace's son.

The Wombourne Institute, Church Road. This was built in 1833 as a school, paid for by Mrs Sarah Dalton of Lloyd House. In 1863 it became the Institute, a place for debates, lectures and meetings. Among its many twentieth-century uses was that of village clinic. In the 1970s it was enlarged. It now houses a day-care centre, parish office, volunteer bureau and gatherings of all kinds. The motto over the porch, 'Lets go hand in hand together, not one before another', was put up by the founders of the Institute, and is still the aim of those who use it now.

The way to school, 1892. In ancient documents this was 'the way to Bobbington', in 1808 'Wombourne Lane'. In praise of the new vicarage in 1835 it became Vicarage Road, and pride in its new National School made it School Lane Road in 1863. Village school education was anything but behind the times – this one had a 'babies class' for three-year-olds by 1893.

John Apse, schoolmaster from 1908 to 1946, and one of the village's first cars. John Apse came from Somerset with a young wife, had a year at Claverley, and then gave the rest of his life to Wombourne School, the church and community. Respected by all ages, his name goes on in Apse Close and the Apse Gate, the north entrance to the churchyard opposite his old and much loved school.

School bee-keeping, c. 1913. John Apse was an expert at bee-keeping, winning prizes in local and county shows. The children enjoyed it too, especially getting the honey out of the combs, because there was always plenty to lick off their fingers! The curriculum included every subject necessary for country life, and not many pupils left without a good grounding in house, garden and family care. There was even a poultry-keeping class, for few houses were without a fowl pen in the garden. John Apse's assistant master is at the back, far right.

Netball shield winners, 1922. Front row, left to right: Beryl Jones, Jessie Ford, Elita Corns, Millicent Bourne. Back row, left to right: John Apse, Harriet Corns, Ruth Davies, Molly Deans, Miss Lewis. They played against schools as far away as Brierley Hill. The awards were presented at the drill hall in Newhampton Road, Wolverhampton.

The 1st XI football team, 1920/1. Back row, left to right: Revd Cox (curate), John Apse, George Rogers, Revd H.L. Langley. Middle row, left to right: ? Banbery, -?-, Tommy Jones, -?-, ? Barrett, ? Woodall. Third row, left to right: W. Rogers, -?-, -?-, Jack Apse, Harry Cartwright. Front row, left to right: Fred Holder, Ken Corns. Revd Cox lived in the present Wombourne Institute and Revd H.L. Langley was vicar of Wombourne (1916–36).

Christmas parcels for the old boys who were away at the First World War. John Apse and his staff had reason to be proud of the youngsters' efforts. His assistant master (see bottom picture, p. 69) was 'away at the war' at this time, and sadly did not survive to return to Wombourne.

The School Choir, 1927. Back row, left to right: Elsie Banbery, Phylis ?, Una Abel, Mary Spark, Eunice Piper, Jack Holder, Stan Johnson, -?-, -?-. Second row, left to right: Edna Norwood, Kathy Hopcut, Edna Perry, ? Cresswell, ? Williams, -?-, George Massey, Cyril Evans, -?-, -?-. Third row, left to right: ? Rowlands, Gwen Bennett, Ivy Guest, Kathy Bullock, -?-, Ted Corns, -?-, -?-, -?-, -?-. Front row, left to right: Hilda Hobbs, Nancy Witherford, Gwen Corns, Bob Key, Sam Dyehouse, Dennis Williams, Dennis Morrell.

The beginners' class in the Wolverhampton Folk Dance competition, 1927. These were the second prize winners. Back row, left to right: Hilda Butcher, Muriel Carrier, Hilda Cresswell, Frances Jones. Front row, left to right: Elsie Tomlinson, Muriel Corns, Hilda Hayward, Florence Banbery. They were aged seven to nine. Most of the school photographs were taken on the 'Rec', the local name for the public open space opposite the school building, now part of the churchyard. The lovely elms behind the children were a feature of the road.

Standard Two infants, all aged six. Each day they had sums, spellings, dictation, writing and reading, and a test every week, as the author (the one with a bow on her head) well remembers. The girl far left is Louise Davies, the boy next to her is Norman Jones, and Dorothy Moore is in the middle of the second row.

Country dancing on the school lawn, 1932. Front row, left to right: Agnes Spiller, May Jones, Winnie Rogers, Margaret Harris, Doris Haynes. Dolly Dyehouse is far left, back; Elsie Leech is behind Margaret Harris. Pickrells Hill is in the background. John Apse taught the boys every aspect of gardening, and the fruit and vegetables they grew were used in the girls' cookery class taught by his wife. On good days the lawn was used for other lessons as well as dancing.

The village school. This has been replaced by a more easily heated and managed building. It had nearly a century of young Wombourne through its doors, serving them well, and many mourned its passing. But bricks and mortar do not make a school good; it was the staff and pupils together. The iron cross from the roof is now on the wall of the new school and the bell is in the foyer, bridging the gap between the old and the new.

The Congregational Chapel, Mill Lane, c. 1890. This is now the United Reformed Church. It was built in 1851 by non-conformists who met previously in rooms at Lower End and has been altered and enlarged since. The hall at the back was added in 1957 by A.J. Allen of Greenhill House, in memory of his wife. The little spire was removed in 1914.

Anniversary day, 1929. Back row, left to right: visiting minister, Geoff Dark (organist), Bill Guest, Eric Corns, Henry Thomas (church superintendent), ? Elcock, Leonard Bennett, George Cartwright, Harold Moore, Leslie Dunn, ? Rack, Bill Evans, Aubrey Williams, Mr Rack (conductor). Middle row, left to right: Muriel Corns, Mary Dyehouse, Dorothy Dunn, Elsie Rowley, Mary Guest, Beatrice Fletcher, Florence Banbery, Hannah King, Edith Rowlands, Jean Oakley. Third row, left to right: -?-, -?-, -?-, Dorothy Evans, Dorothy Moore, Daphne Allen, Hazel Hopcutt, Dolly Dyehouse, Doris Hewitt, -?-, Dolly Guest, Florence Tranter. Front row, left to right: John Thomas, John Hale, George Thomas.

On the vicarage lawn, 1923. The Revd H.L. Langley is with a solid bank of Mothers' Union members, to whom quite a few present Wombourne people are related. Like its contemporaries, the old vicarage house was large and the garden reached from School Road to High Street. It was a pleasant place and just right for such gatherings.

The Wombourne Choral Society, 1936. It swept the board in the county competitions by winning eight awards. It was founded in 1929 by Harry England (third left, front row), who retired to Netley House in the Bull Ring after twenty-seven years as head of Enville School. Its traditions have been carried on in the Wombourne and District Choral Society, and the excellent standards set by its founder still continue.

The bottom of Mill Lane, *c.* 1950. Records show that there has been a water mill here on the Wom Brook for many centuries. It was already ancient by the sixteenth century and was both a corn and a blade mill. It ended as the latter in the late nineteenth century the premises of T. Meredith, a scythe manufacturer.

Sandy Lane, *c.* 1900. This is now parish public footpath no. 27 from Rookery Road (at the Lower End entrance to Redclyffe Drive) to Green Hill. It used to go diagonally across the field to a stile opposite the Sytch Lane but now, since the land was developed, ends in the Copper Beech Drive. It got its name from a late eighteenth-century sand quarry in the hillside on the right (behind Park Mount), the earliest recorded mining area in the village. This view is down the lane towards Rookery Road.

Daniel Rogers and family outside their home in Rookery Road. This ancient cottage was typical of local workmen's dwellings before the eighteenth century. Like its contemporaries it had a huge garden, a pigsty and a fowlpen, each of which helped provide good food all the year round. Daniel, as his father Daniel before him, was an excellent bricklayer, and built three houses on the site of his old cottage (see far right, top picture, p. 78). Here he is with his wife and their four children, George, Eva, Eliza Ann and Frances.

Daniel Rogers and his wife outside their home.

The Lower End, 1950. The land around the junction of Common Road, Green Hill, Gravel Hill and Rookery Road takes its name from the nearby 'nether' or 'lower' bridge over the Wom Brook. The white building on the left in the foreground was the non-conformist meeting house before 1851 (see p. 74, top picture). The space between the next house and the dormer-windowed almshouses was the village pound. The large white house was a nail warehouse in 1851. The next detached cottage was a nailer's home and workshop. The row of three cottages on the far right replaced the Rogers's cottage (p. 77). The flat field in front of the houses was used for football until built over in the 1980s. The central portion opposite the large white house was Catherine's Croft before 1800 and had two cottages on it.

The road junction at the Lower End. Gravel Hill House is in the far centre and the old maltings are on the left.

The Mill Farm, Common Road, late 1930s. This is on the site of an ancient water mill, used for corn but adapted for armaments during the civil wars in the mid-seventeenth century. The name 'Hammer Mill' stuck and the meadow behind as far as the brook bridge was still Ham Mill Meadow and Pool in the late nineteenth century. There was a footpath from Common Road across the meadow in front of the house which continued along the brook to Giggetty, once the way to the mill and now part of the Wom Brook Walk.

The Longlands from Common Road to the brook, 1960s. At least five centuries ago all the land from the present Ounsdale Road to 'The Sitch' was Blakeley open field. What is now Common Road was a track through it to the common land beyond the present Giggetty Lane. This field was about to be built on and in its last summer, instead of producing a good grain crop, was one mass of poppies.

Wombourne Common, 1920s. Blakeley and Wombourne Common are the same place. When the commons were enclosed after 1808 and a small hamlet grew up near Blakeley field, both names were used quite officially, depending on the whim of the writer. This view was from close to the present entrance to Wombourne Park looking northwards.

Wombourne Common Methodist Church, c. 1954. After meeting for some years in a cottage opposite the above building, now the site of Wesley Close, the Methodists had premises in Chapel Street. In 1894 this church was built and has been enlarged considerably since. The present minister cares also for Springdale Church at Penn and the little one at Gospel Ash near Halfpenny Green. The old laburnums were felled in the late 1980s.

This group knew how to work hard and play hard and they are waiting for a modern 1920s charabanc to whisk them away for a few hours, farther than they could go in a horse-drawn bus. Their overcoats, caps and mackintoshs were in place, and little short of an earthquake would have turned them back.

The Masons Arms, Blakeley/Wombourne Common, *c.* 1899. The common boasted two pubs with a Methodist church in between. This pub sold its last pint in the early twentieth century and is now two takeaways – one for fish and chips and one for Chinese food. These are a far cry from the tiny bar with two big wooden settles to keep away draughts and a spittoon in the corner.

The Pattmore family came from Somerset in the mid-nineteenth century. With the Hughes family and others, they were prominent members of the Methodist Church. This shop had changed little by the 1930s. Among its pleasures were children's favourites such as liquorice shoelaces, gobstoppers and yellow kali which stained mouths, fingers and clothes bright yellow.

Planks Lane looking towards Black Hill, 1950. Narrow and winding, with hedges on top of high banks and wild flowers of all kinds in their seasons, this was typical of most ways into Wombourne. 'Planke' is an old word for a piece of land of about an acre, which is longer than it is broad. It referred to seven narrow fields that reached from the present Ounsdale Road to the top end of Planks Lane. The gate is in the position of the present butchers shop.

This house in Planks Lane has been replaced by no. 103. It had the nickname of 'Giggetty Hall', and its last owners were John Halpin and his wife. He was a parish councillor and both of them were friends in need to many people. The pleasant garden was full of flowers and produce, and there was poultry of all kinds in the paddock across the brook.

The Boat Inn, Botterham, *c*. 1900. It is many years since the landlord last called 'time', but the premises with stabling and warehouse attached have survived. The photographer was standing with his back to Swindon village, almost at the point where the boundary with Wombourne crosses the canal. At roughly the same place today a large pipe goes over it, carrying water from a storage reservoir near the River Severn at Hampton Loade to an enclosed reservoir on top of Sedgley Beacon. Botterham, the 'settlement at the bottom of the valley', was a pleasant place for workers and walkers at the turn of the century. Thankfully it still is, even without a jug of ale and a bench in the sun.

Botterham, *c.* 1900. There is one bridge (no. 42 on the canal) and two locks (nos. 20 and 21, the numbering begins at the southern end), and the land fall is 20 ft. The Staffordshire and Worcestershire Canal was opened in 1772. It connects the River Severn at Stourport with the Trent and Mersey Canal at Great Haywood near Stafford. It was planned by James Brindley and is a contour canal: its forty-six miles follow the valleys of the Stour, Smestow and Penk rivers, winding gently like a natural waterway. A bridle path (Wombourne parish path no. 38) goes from the locks to the Bridgnorth Road (B4176) close to the crossroads to Swindon. The lock-house has had some alterations. A couple of other cottages just below on the same side were demolished in the mid-twentieth century.

The Canal Watch House and stable, Giggetty. This was built in the late eighteenth century. The Stafford and Worcester Canal was very busy, so that the towing path had no time to grow over. No sooner had one loaded boat passed than another came. Nevertheless, there was time for fishing and boating, and most of the youngsters learned to swim in the canal without harm.

The Canal Watch House. Left to right: Nellie Critchley and her aunt, Elizabeth Critchley.

Giggetty Bridge, 1950s. This is James Brindley's original bridge (no. 44), built of strong brick with wide stone coping. The present, late twentieth-century bridge is ugly in comparison and certainly no wider. Here the height was perfect for sitting or leaning, the stone for carving initials and hearts, and only a rare vehicle disturbed the peaceful pastime of watching the boats go by. The young lady is Shirley Cowern.

The footbridge at Dickies Brook (or, correctly, Longford), c. 1908. Here the Wom Brook has just come under the canal and is about to be joined by a smaller stream whch rises on Goldthorn Hill. Edith May Critchley (the author's mother) and her sister, Alice Isabella, are trying to fool everyone into thinking they had a three-wheeler Sunbeam bicycle.

Sand Quarries, Giggetty Lane, *c.* 1930. Critchley's sand 'pit' is at the back of the present houses nos. 98 to 101. The hedge is alongside the garden of Holly Cottage. It was good-quality sand and gravel and went all over the Midlands by canal.

'Wombourne by the sea', 1958. This was in a quarry now under houses on the Pool House Estate. It was sheltered and safe, with six-inch deep, clear, clean water. Bulrushes, meadow sweet, a picnic and all the sand a child needed made it a paradise.

Giggetty Bridge (no. 44) looking towards Ounsdale, 1920. There were at least seven small wharfs in the parish, and the one by this bridge mostly handled coal and sand. The occupants of the cottages (right) lost most of their gardens when the canal was built. The Round Oak at Ounsdale is near the horizon by the big tree.

Ounsdale, 1950s. Many of the old houses have been replaced. The hamlet grew up after the canal came through in the late nineteenth century. The name is a corruption of 'Holendene', 'a little valley where holly grew'. The locals call it 'Houndel', and that is what is on bridge no. 45. The left-hand cottage in the row was a pub called the Navigation which preceded the present Round Oak and Mount Pleasant close by.

The Bratch Locks (nos. 23, 24, and 25) and two bridges (nos. 47 and 48). The southern portion of the canal was begun in 1766 at the summit at Compton. At first the landfall was slight; at Bratch it was 30 ft in so many yards. The flight of three deep locks was a major engineering work, and later needed reconstruction. The octagonal toll house is the oldest of its type surviving on this canal.

The Bratch Pumping Station, c. 1897. The town of Bilston badly needed a new water supply and there was plenty to spare in the Smestow valley. The villagers of Wombourne complained that if a bore went ahead their wells would go dry. They were proved right and their anger was not appeased until they too had piped water and a discount on their bills. The pumping station is a listed building in red brick, with red, buff and blue decoration and a castellated engine house with four corner turrets.

The Waterworks House in Bratch Lane, looking eastward before the railway building began in 1913. The long, steep bank below the woods at Bull Meadow was known as The Butts and was long ago the place for shooting practice (with bows and arrows). A long, wooden chalet just beyond the house was known locally as The Bilston Children's Holiday Camp and provided children from that town with a few days 'in the country'.

The Seisdon Union Isolation Hospital, Bratch Common Road, *c*. 1900. Infectious diseases like small pox and diphtheria were common. This small hospital had room for twenty-four patients who stayed sometimes as long as three months. Visitors could only speak to them through a hatch. Known locally as the 'fever hospital', it closed in the mid-twentieth century and was made into two dwellings.

The Wom Brook at Wodehouse Mill is fed by springs from Spring Hill, Lloyd Hill and Colton Hills, and joins the Smestow just below Heath Mill Road. The fast streams of the Smestow valley were harnessed from early times, providing power for numerous mills and forges. Wombourne had four mills in little over a mile: at Wodehouse, Mill Lane, Lower End and at the Heath. This was a fine record for such a short distance.

Heath Mills Pool, 1930. The Heath took extra water by leat from the Smestow in Trysull. This pool was recorded as 'new' in the late eighteenth century. The old pool on the Wom Brook was beyond the horizon on lower ground. It was a local beauty spot, lost when it was drained in the 1940s. A workman's cottage, the 'Pool House', gave its name to the nearby road, and in the late twentieth century to a large housing estate.

Heath Mill, 1940. The ancient mill was remodelled by Lord Wrottesley in 1827 and converted to a corn mill. It stopped working *c.* 1930. In the seventeenth century the site was worked by Thomas Foley and his son Philip as an iron forge, together with Swin Forge and Greens Forge (then in Wombourne Parish). All three sites are thought to have been used by iron pioneer Dud Dudley while experimenting at smelting iron with coal. The road names of the nearby estate were chosen to reflect its important ancient history and land use.

Heath House, *c.* 1920. This was built in the early eighteenth century about 60 yds north of the mill on the far edge of 'Womborne Hethe', with terraced gardens dropping to a small pool surrounded by many beautiful trees. In the 1970s the elegant service wings were demolished, the main house became flats, and the name it had had for two hundred and fifty years was lost when it became Mansion Court.

Threshing at Orton, *c.* 1890. Agriculture and horticulture flourished on Wombourne's light sandy soil. Even during the brief period of domestic hand-made nail-making in the mid-nineteenth century, most labouring families did seasonal work in the fields. Everyone joined in, and the schoolmaster had great difficulty getting the children to lessons when they could earn money on the land. He had to adjust the summer holiday dates to suit the harvest season.

Ted Cowern with two friends, outside Providence Cottages in Giggetty Lane, *c.* 1923. Until fifty years ago, good heavy horses meant a good farm, and who can resist their quiet dignity and restrained power even today?

Green Hill Farm, 1901. In 1800 the way to this house was a track from Green Hill along 'The Sitch'. After the nearby common was enclosed in 1808, the owner, Robert Dickenson (his name is perpetuated in Dickenson Road), had a private carriageway down to the growing hamlet of Blakeley. This is now the right-angle arm of the present Sytch Lane. 'Sitch' is an old word for 'boundary', in this case between the arable land and the waste land.

Green Hill House, built *c.* 1835, now part of the small estate of Green Hill Gardens. This was the mid-nineteenth-century home of A.J. Allen (see p. 74) and in the late nineteenth century of George Addenbrooke, an ironmaster, who called it Addenbrooke House.

The Townsend, from Birch Hill behind the Red Lion, *c.* 1900. From left to right, near the horizon: Arbour Tree House, the church spire, Waverley Farm (now the police station), the Vine, a shop and house (now a car park), the Old Bush (see p. 58) and the Small Brook Houses. The old blind arches of Rushford Bridge are clear, but are now hidden by trees. Before the nineteenth century the drive from the Wodehouse lay on high ground on the east of the brook, reaching the road at what is now the Red Lion car park. It is pinpointed here by the dark line of turf. The names Rushford, Townsend and Birch Hill were in use before the fourteenth century.

Wombourne Showground, 1950. The show moved to the Townsend meadows in 1925 and grew steadily in size and reputation. At first it was the gardeners, WI members and friends who ran it. After the Second World War they were joined by the Cricket, Tennis and Bowls Club, and for a few years by the Civil Defence Club (now Wombourne Club). It took a year on paper to organize a week on the ground – some members had to help get the hay off it first. On the day, eight to ten thousand people came through the gate. Car parking was on the Small Brook fields. It was a day for meeting old friends and making new ones, but rising costs of tentage and printing (plus a few other reasons) brought an end to a show on this scale on these fields.

The village fête, 1922. This was held on the cricket field and was a revival of the show tradition. Harold Gittins, John Apse, other interested gardeners, and the newly formed WI members ran it, and there was to be no looking back. The newspaper report filled a long column – almost everyone in the village seemed to have been there.

The village fête. The WI members' entry in the decorated cart competition. The horse (in the picture above) looks strong enough to pull them, so no doubt all was well. Mrs Shaw Hellier is about to perform the opening ceremony. The Cottages in High Street are just visible behind the crowd.

The village fête, *c.* 1960. This is the first year after the move to the fields near Gilbert Lane and shows the fancy dress parade in front of the Small Brook cottages. An old house, Sandy Mount, is just visible on the top right.

The village fête, *c.* 1960. This is in a hundred foot marquee which contained the Open Class exhibits, attracting entries from nurseries and large country houses. There were two more for the villagers entries and another for the children's. Special buses ran from nearby towns. Although the beer tent was open all day, hooliganism was non-existent – just the site of a calm constable walking round was enough. Any arguments were usually confined to who thought who should have won, and who shouldn't have who did! Left to right: May Griffiths, Ken Rock, John Apse.

At the fête, the horse jumping was run strictly to British Show Jumping Association rules – jumps meticulously constructed and timing equipment perfect. Vet, farrier, doctor and nurses were on hand. Riders came from all over the Midland counties. There were intervals for other ring entertainment, such as sheep-dog trials, motor cycle displays and acrobats.

The fête wasn't all flowers, horses, sideshows and the beer tent. At about half-past five, the ring was cleared and gentlemen from Cradley Heath and its environs set up a race course for their whippets. Ticktack men and bookies appeared, seemingly from nowhere, and the villagers took advantage. The show was a 'day out at home', and the more variety, the more there was to remember.

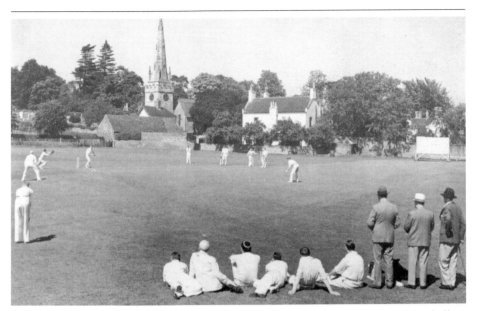

It was a perfect Saturday in early July 1935 and the 2nd XI were playing Blakenhall. A *Times* photographer captured the moment and his picture has appeared in several national publications since, including adverts for the Standard Motor Company in the 1950s. The old sandstone church still stands firm, but the manor house was replaced by a modern clubhouse in 1969. The old name for the land is Dovecote Close. The cricket scene is still part of Wombourne life, whatever else may have changed.

The Ist XI, 1913. Back row, left to right: Umpire Mansell, ? Longbottom, E. Sadler, J. Crumpton, ? Hickman, R. Rogers, H. Sadler, ? Tongue. Middle row, left to right: T. Johnson, C. Sadler, C. Fletcher, Hiram Carrier, J. Beddena, B. Alcock, G.W. Watts. Front row, left to right: John Smith, Len Hayward.

The cricket team travel to an away match. The journeys by horse brake must have been encountered with good humour, for anyone who fell out might easily fall off as well. Even though the cricket was a serious matter, the tea afterwards, the fellowship and the trip home were as much a part of the day out as the battle that had just been fought.

The horse that pulled the roller and the mowing machine for the cricket and hockey pitches. There was a gentler hand-mower for the wicket, the tennis courts and the bowling green. In 1910 the groundsman asked whether, if he provided his own horse, he could let it out on the field. The committee's answer was an emphatic 'No'.

Tennis players, 1913. Back row, left to right: Elsie Beddard, Harry Graves, Mrs Mobberley. Next row, left to right: Mr Gay, Muriel Cartwright, Mrs Gay, Lola Cartwright, Mrs May, Mr May. Third row, left to right: -?-, -?-, -?-, Horace Sadler, Mrs Hughes, -?-, Ernie Sadler. Front row, left to right: Mr Hughes, Mrs Sayer, Clem Sadler, Mrs Clem Sadler, Mr Harper, Mrs Horace Sadler, John Apse, Florence Apse.

The bowling team, *c.* 1930. Back row, left to right: ? Rogers, Will Jones, ? Bennett, A. Jenks, H. Hayward, John Apse, A. Banbery, W. Deve, Tom Guest. Front row, left to right: Mr Barrett, Joseph Corns, George Rogers, John Halpin, P.G. Banbery. Mr Jenks saw fit to keep his hat on. He was council chairman as well as a bowling man. Jenks Road perpetuates the many years of community service he and his family gave to the village.

Members of the hockey club, *c.* 1912. This was at the beginning of the club's association with Wombourne. Some local men were in the teams, but they were mostly drawn from outside the area, hockey being a game played more at colleges than at the village schools. The games were played on the Maypole Street side of the ground. After the Second World War, the club moved to their present site in Pendeford Lane, Wolverhampton, but they still keep their old Wombourne name.

A hockey match in progress, *c.* 1912.

This football team won the 1919/20 Wolverhampton District Church and Chapel League championship. Back row, left to right: Billy Day, Jack Carrier, George Jordan, George Walker, George Guest, Henry Bassano, Frank Crowe, George Piper, James Spark, Front row, left to right: Fred Cartwright, Arthur Hooks, Len Collins, Arthur Piper (later played for Wolves), Ben Webb.

This football team was in the 1947/8 Wolverhampton Amateur League. Back row, left to right: Geoff Piper, Bill Evans, Desmond Piper, George Hayden, Barry Rogers, Alan Breakwell (later played for Wolves), Ron Piper, Jack Breakwell, Allan Blakeway, W. Vaughan, Front row, left to right: Tommy Vaughan, ? George, ? Thomas, Ken Piper, Tommy Danks, Gordon Guest.

Drumhead Service, March 1920. 'On Sunday afternoon, a drumhead service in memory of the lads who have fallen, promoted by the National Association of Discharged Sailors and Soldiers was held on the cricket ground, over 500 being present. A parade under the command of Lt-Col. Carter DSO, MC, proceeded from the Arbour Tree to the ground headed by the Federation Band, the service there was conducted by the Revd H. Langley MA, vicar of Wombourne. Afterwards the parade marched to the churchyard where wreaths were laid on the graves of local men who had died in the service of their country. The last post was sounded, prayers were said by the vicar, the buglers sounded the reveille, thus bringing to a close a very momentous occasion in the history of the village' (*Wolverhampton Chronicle*).

The Territorials were as ready in peace as they had been in war time. One of the 1930s training camps was in Himley Park. The young man, third from the right in the back row, is Weyman Jones of Common Road, who was the farrier. The efficient care of the horses was a vital factor in the army. Weyman could turn his hand to many trades, and this was just one of them.

Churchill said, 'We will defend our island', and not the least of those who rallied were the Home Guard. Wombourne men were in B Company, 24th Staffordshire Battalion, and much of their training took place in Patshull Park.

A wartime concert, *c.* 1942. The youngsters are enjoying a Punch and Judy show in the Manor House yard outside the stables. There is just a glimpse of the house at the bottom of Love Alley.

Some of the youngsters of Wombourne, 1941. In the early years of the war, the *Express and Star* ran a club for young people. It was morale boosting, interest forming and fun. At the very front is Jill Walker. Next row, left to right: Celia Abbiss, Mary Riley, June Deadman, Rosamund Moore, Margaret Walker, Ann Fellows, Lorna Oaks. Third row, left to right: Betty Wood, Mrs Foster (who ran the group), Margaret Foster, Reg Johnson. Back row, left to right: Beryl Bull, Ann Lewis.

Winter came with a vengeance in early 1947. This view is from Wodehouse Lane corner, looking up Small Brook Lane. There was snow on snow on snow, and the girls are standing at the level of the hedge top. Drifts were as high as first-floor windows. The road to Sedgley was blocked just beyond the Wodehouse by a snow-buried single-decker bus. The A449 at Withymore was under 6 ft of frozen snow and it took three days to dig a single track through.

The 'Old Staffs and Worcs' canal had several feet of ice. It could have supported a tank, let alone May Griffiths. The extreme conditions went on for several weeks, and people wondered if spring would ever come again. It did, and was followed by one of the hottest summers on record. Just discernible in the distance on the right are the original crane houses by the track down to Heath Mill.

Outside the almshouses in Rookery Road. From the reign of Queen Elizabeth I, each parish had to care for its own sick and poor people, and most built a few houses for the purpose. Some of Wombourne's almshouses still exist in Rookery Road, although they are now privately owned. They bear a stone tablet with the date 1716 and the Jesus' words, 'The Poor ye have Alway' (John 12:8). The pretty children in the picture lived nearby at the beginning of this century.

St Benedict Biscop Church, c. 1900. The south wall glowed with virginia creeper and five copper beech trees graced the front wall. Two of these trees remain in the 1990s. The postman and the cyclist were wise enough to find time 'to stand and stare'. The old elm was already dying, and soon its great branches would begin to drop.

Trysull and Seisdon

Trysull Village in quieter days. The Bell Inn is on the left, the church tower behind it and the former Village Institute, built by B.H. Mander of the Manor House in 1896, is on the right.

A view of Trysull Village from North Hill before the end of the nineteenth century when the Institute was built opposite the church. The Bell Inn is on the left. In the foreground is the Mill House, beyond which are two small cottages which still stand in The Holloway. The second cottage used to house the village post office.

Trysull Village from the south, another general view taken at the same time. Immediately to the left of the church is Trysull House, while to the right is the front of a house which

This is the third in a set of views of Trysull Village, this time looking from the north-west. Trysull House is in front of and to the right of the church. The house on the extreme right is believed to be The Laurels.

appears to have been demolished when the Institute was built. (The back of this house is to the right of the Bell in the picture above.)

A 'chocolate box' view of The Holloway dating from the early years of the twentieth century. This reflects the nature of the area as a tourist resort for Wolverhampton and the towns of the Black Country. This photograph was also used as a postcard. Trysull Mill House is in the background on the left. The two houses on the right, which appear to date from the same time as the Institute, still stand, although the wall and trees have gone. The Institute, which has recently been used as a restaurant, is now a private house.

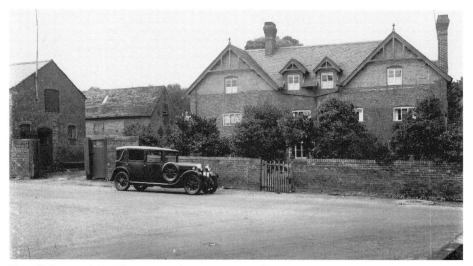

Trysull Farm, 1929. This is now known as Trysull House and very little has changed on the outside. The farm was then owned by Lord Wrottesley and the tenant was Mr James Marsh.

Trysull Manor House, late 1940s. It is not clear if this is the original manor house, but it has been known by this name since 1860. It was occupied by the Jesson family for most of the nineteenth century. It was then bought by Howard Benjamin Mander in 1894, remaining in the possession of the Mander family until 1940. A famous visitor to the house was Samuel Johnson. He was brought to stay there in 1711 as an infant. The house has often been used as the venue for village functions, and this view was taken during a WI summer fête.

The Cottage, now known as Four Ways, is on the left, with an unusual view of the church. The village schoolmaster, John Salmon, moved here in 1924 after retiring from teaching.

The Laurels, home of the Granger family, stood in Seisdon Road on the site of the present group of bungalows. Many of the nineteenth-century views of Trysull included in this book were taken by a man who lodged here. When he died he left his collection of very professional photographs in the possession of the Granger family. Sadly his name is not known. Mrs Granger stands in the doorway, the girl is Alice Granger and the boy is believed to be a younger brother who died in his teens. One of the rooms in the house was once used as the village gaol and then later as the village shop.

The Weir, Trysull Mill. Smestow Brook is to the left while the two boys sit on the sluice gate which controlled the flow of water into the mill leat. The mill stands to the west of Trysull bridge in Church Lane. The pool lay behind Trysull Farm parallel to the Seisdon Road. The mill is in the background.

Trysull Tea Gardens, Feiashill Road. This is a further indication of the early tourist trade in this area. The board in the garden reads, 'Mr Evans: Teas provided on the shortest notice'. The cottage, which still stands near the junction with Crockington Lane, was later occupied by the village schoolmaster, John Salmon, and his family. It is now known as Little Green.

Woodford Grange. This house stands on or near the site of a much older house which belonged to Dudley Priory in the twelfth century. As it was a monastic site it was not part of any parish until added to Trysull in 1900. Early in the seventeenth century it passed into the hands of the Wrottesley family and was apparently used as a dower house for a time. In later years the Woodford Estate comprised this house together with a farm and cottage. In 1929, when Lord Wrottesley put part of his estate up for sale, the Grange was sold along with several other properties in Trysull and Seisdon.

Members of the Girls' Friendly Society pose for a photograph while on a picnic, sometime
c. 1905–10. The girl seated in the middle row, third from the left, is Alice Granger. Many
such societies existed in the Midlands. They were run by middle-class ladies for working-
class girls. Their aim was to encourage the girls to develop desirable qualities, such as
sobriety and respect for their betters, that would enable them to become good servants.

Trysull Mothers' Union, 1906. Mrs Granger is seated second from the left.

Members of the Trees Lodge outside the Plough Inn, *c.* 1896. This is when Charles Whitmore Munday is recorded in Kelly's Trade Directory as maltster and farmer of the Plough Inn. The Plough dates back to at least 1834. The United Order of Free Gardeners, a Friendly Society, met at the Plough from 1870.

Members of the Spanish Royal family gather outside Trysull Manor House, prior to joining members of the Mander family for a meeting of the Albrighton Hunt. The date is believed to be 1929. The royal visitors were Queen Ena and her two daughters, the Infantas. They were guests at Himley Hall.

The British Legion outside the Bell Inn.

Wolverhampton Naturalist and Archaeological Society on a visit to Trysull, 20 June 1896.
The trip was recorded in the society's scrapbook. The 1896 programme stated that Col.
Thorneycroft had kindly placed his barge at their disposal and would join the excursion.
The paper was to be read by Mr B. Turton. Tea would be taken at Trysull with Col.
Thorneycroft's band in attendance. The boat was to start from Newbridge at 3 p.m.
sharp. It is to be hoped that they did not all travel on the one boat!

All Saints Church, Trysull, some time after the restoration of the tower in 1897. The clock was replaced and a new peal of bells hung, which made it difficult to use the west door and resulted in the construction of a new south porch.

The interior of All Saints some time before 1897 when the pulpit was moved to the other side of the chancel arch. The most unusual bequest associated with the church was that of John Rudge. In 1722 he left 20s. a year to pay for a 'sleeparouser'. This person had to patrol the church during services to wake up any people who had dozed off. Men were woken with the knob end of a pole while a feather on the other end was employed to tickle the ladies awake!

The old school and schoolmaster's house. The original school building stood near to the church and was founded in 1707 with money given by Thomas Rudge of Westminster. The income from land at Trimpley bought with his £200 endowment was used to teach eighteen poor children of the parish, chosen by trustees. In 1843 the building here was built on land given by Lord Wrottesley to accommodate 130 children. The master's house on the left was added in the mid-1860s.

Boys from the school enjoy a tug of war, on the Green, supervised by the schoolmaster, John Offley William Salmon. Mr Salmon began teaching at the school on 2 April 1883 after training at St Peters training college, Saltley, Birmingham. By 1899, two of his sons, J.T. (Tom) and Charles, were teaching in the school and Tom took over from his father as schoolmaster in 1924. Tom's wife also taught sewing in the school before they were married.

The three Salmon boys in the school garden. Left to right: Tom, Bill, Charles.

Damage caused to the school on Sunday 24 March 1895, when a violent storm led to the collapse of the chimney and bell turret. At first, all the children had to be taught in the infants' room. By June the parish magazine was reporting that 'the whole school will have to be rebuilt'.

John Salmon with a group of pupils outside the new school building, c. 1908–09. The lady teacher is Miss Summers who later became Mrs Binschadler. She was also matron of the Seisdon workhouse. This building was opened in 1896, paid for by a bequest from Eliza Baker, formerly of Seisdon.

The school garden. When the new school was built it was provided with a garden to enable horticulture to be taught and 'enhance the usefulness of the school'. John Salmon had a keen interest in horticulture and developed the garden to a very high standard. He began selling flowers commercially while still the schoolmaster, and when he retired opened Trysull Flower Farm. In 1900 he experimented with turning surplus damsons into wine and became the first person in the country to be licensed to sell home-produced wines. By 1925 he was producing and selling wine on quite a large scale.

Trysull School, 1924. The schoolmaster is Mr Tom Salmon.

Trysull School, 1940. The pupils on the left of the main group are the infants' class. The girls in the other classes are: Marion Whele, Mary Taylor, Joyce Owen, Joyce Coxsill, Eileen Guest, May Reynolds, Joan Cole, Sylvia Davis, Jean Coxsill, Pat Edwards, Gladys Upton, Joyce Fazey, Margery Guest, Barbara Guest, Brenda Owen, Pauline Stephens, Gladys Littleford, Edith Baxter, Betty Frost, Geraldine Hughes, Sylvia Owen, Iris Priest, Betty Stephens, Doris Law, Eileen Upton, Elsa Fazey, Margery Evans, Eileen Cowern, Peggy Cowern, Joan Thomas, Ruth Slater, Kathleen Perkins, Miriam Cole, Ena Walker, Maud Hartshorne, Gladys Butler, Joan Frost, Margaret Taylor, Jean McKlacklan, Jean Link, Phylis Corns, Margaret Cresswell, Betty Fazey, Thelma Badger, June Massey, Jean Morgan, Jean Clinton and Anita Hollick.

Four photographs depicting rural scenes in this area were taken by the photographer that lodged with the Grangers. They appear to have been entered in a photographic competition. This one was captioned, 'Oxen ploughing at Trysull, part of First Prize Photographic Set, Farm Field and Fireside May 13th 1898'.

'Reaping Wheat Trysull' was the title for this view, which was also part of the first prize set.

'Sheep Shearing at Woodford.' This is one of a set of studies of sheep shearing.

'Afternoon Tea in the Hayfield': a rather posed photograph of Mr Walling's men. Mr William Walling owned land and farmed at Beech House, later known as Beech Farm or The Beeches, which stands at the end of a lane leading from Crockington Lane. The 1896 Kelly's Trade Directory places Beech House in Trysull, while the 1924 edition, which also names William Walling as the occupier, places it in Seisdon.

Trysull Mill as it appeared in the sale catalogue of 1929. This building dates from 1854. It replaced an earlier mill which occupied the same site at least as early as 1775 when it was shown on Yates's Map of Staffordshire. There was a mill in Trysull at the time of Domesday, though its location is not known. This building was apparently bought from Lord Wrottesley by his tenant in 1929 and continued in use until 1950. It lay derelict for many years but is now restored and used as a private residence. The pool has now gone.

Trysull Mill House stands on the corner of the Holloway and Church Lane. This view is also taken from the sale catalogue where house, mill and outbuildings, osier beds, two arable fields, three acres of pasture and the pool all formed one lot.

Trysull Smithy, *c.* 1898. The smithy, which still stands in the Holloway near to the bridge, was built around this date. The building has been extended and is now used as a garage. The blacksmith in 1896 was John Murray, who is probably the man on the right here. The village had another smithy which stood in School Road near the pound, just to the north of the green.

Trysull Flower Farm. Charles Salmon stands with his wife and son, John, in a field of arum lilies, *c.* 1925. The growing of arum lilies out of doors was developed by Charles and his father, and they sold cut blooms direct to florists all over the Midlands, winning prizes at local flower shows. A bed of lilies from the nursery has been planted in the Garden of Memory at Himley.

The old Seven Stars Inn, Seisdon, stood in front of the present building right on the corner of Tinkers Castle Road (left) and Fox Road (right). The Seven Stars dates back to at least 1714 when the justices held a monthly meeting there. When advertised for sale in 1812 it was described as 'well accustomed' and as having a large clubroom. This view, dating from around the time of the First World War, advertises 'large and small parties catered for' and 'Good bowling green'. The advert on the wall of the club room says 'Teas provided'.

Seisdon Smithy, Ebstree Road. Judging by the lorry this photograph dates from the 1920s. The man standing outside near to the large wheel is presumably the smith who, in 1924, was Albert Oakley. The building, now whitewashed, still stands where the road narrows. The smithy and lean-to have been incorporated into the present house and a porch has been added. Seisdon had two smithies: the second lay farther along Ebstree Road, on the right beyond the bridge.

Seisdon Mill, 1929. The mill stood on Ebstree Road opposite the opening to the Trysull Road, with its mill house and buildings to the right and its pool behind. The mill was bought from Lord Wrottesley by his tenant, W. Banton, a local landowner, in the 1929 sale, along with the house, farm buildings, pool and 'A field of excellent turf land'. The house is dated 1749.

The back of Seisdon mill and mill pool. Seisdon has had a mill since the early thirteenth century. The first mill may have stood on this site. The mill continued to work until *c.* 1950. It was powered by water until electricity was installed in the last ten years of its working life.

Seisdon, looking from the bridge up Ebstree Road towards Wolverhampton, 1950. The junction with Post Office Road is on the left in front of the detached house. The lorry on the right is a Summerton belonging to the Stourbridge Millers, and the Ford car belonged to Miss Joan Jenkins.

Seisdon from the Trysull Road, 1950s. This view is from opposite the front of the Manor House. The black-and-white cottage with the dormer windows is an old cruck cottage, now called Windrush Cottage. The building seen end on is the smithy, with the back of the Laurels and Willowbrook Cottage on the left and extreme left, respectively. On the skyline is the sand quarry off Post Office Road, dating back to the 1930s. A notable feature of the area covered by this book is the sand which has been quarried, at various dates, over much of the region.

A motor-cycle combination outside the Seven Stars. The soldier dates this view to around the time of the First World War. The door to the large clubroom attached to the inn can be seen on the left. The landlord in 1924 was Stephen Brown.

The Seven Stars Bowling Club, *c.* 1920s. The man standing on the far right is the blacksmith, sitting at the front right is Mrs Shotton's father, and in the front row with the buttonhole is Ken Gregory.

The Slate Houses on the corner of Fox Road and Post Office Road. The two ladies in the doorway are Charles Evans' mother and paternal grandmother. Before 1914, these women ran a small business catering for 'Brake' parties travelling from the Black Country for a day out in Bridgnorth.

The tea garden at the rear of the house where the daytrippers could take refreshment.

A group with two working horses outside Meadow Farm, Post Office Road.

Seisdon Rural District Council employees at work on what was then the boundary between Seisdon district and Wolverhampton, at the junction of Trysull Road and Coalway Road. The stone marks the boundary and is on the site of an old water trough. The stone has been repositioned on Langley Road since the boundary was moved.

Swindon, Himley and Baggeridge

Swindon Post Office in the early years of the twentieth century. Although the post office has remained in much the same position, the rest of the High Street has changed out of all recognition. The only building remaining now is the United Reform Church on the right, formerly the Ebenezar Chapel. The advertisement is on the wall of the stables attached to the Old Bush Inn on the corner of Hinksford Lane. The High Street bends sharply round to the left just beyond the post office (right foreground) to become Wolverhampton Road.

Swindon High Street looking towards the Old Bush. The roof of the United Reform Church is in the middle of the houses on the left, and the row of cottages containing the post office is at the top of the hill. The horse and cart are believed to have belonged to a butcher called Mr Fox whose shop was at Gravel Hill, Wombourne. The stables next to the public house were used for horses who had brought deliveries to the steelworks by canal and needed to stay overnight.

Swindon High Street, 1958. This view is looking towards the Old Bush. The large building on the right is Manor House Farm, home of the Reynolds family until it was sold and demolished to make way for a housing development. The gentleman on the left is Mr Alf Clarke who kept the Greyhound, and the lady pushing the pram is Mrs Robinson.

Cottages in the Holloway looking towards the Old Brook Bridge, built by the Earl of Dudley, 1930s or '40s. The terrace was known as Tater Row after a storm washed a crop of potatoes from a field behind right into the houses. The public house is the Green Man on the corner of Church Road. Standing outside the cottage she occupied for many years, in a pinafore, is Mrs Harriet Williams. The cottages were demolished in the 1960s.

The High Street, looking towards the canal bridge, 1950s. The two old cottages were built to house agricultural workers while the row next to them was built for workers at Baldwins Steelworks. The chimney of the works is on the right, and the offices are in the right background. The building in the distance painted white was the Forge Stores.

Manor Farm, one of the few old buildings to remain in the village.

Manor Farm, looking from the Wombourne Road, 1950s. Later, new housing in Albert Drive was built on part of the field. This view was from in front of the houses built by the council in the 1930s to rehouse people from a row of cottages that stood next to the Greyhound.

St John's Parish Church, 1937/8. The church was dedicated in 1854 as a chapel of ease attached to Wombourne. It contained 350 free seats. Swindon became ecclesiastically separate in 1867. The church was built of pink sandstone and stands on a hill to the north of the village.

The interior of St John's when it was still lit by oil lamps. Alterations were made to the interior in the 1930s which involved moving the pulpit and lectern.

The churchyard with the old vicarage behind. The nineteenth-century vicarage has been demolished and a modern building erected on the site, along with several other houses.

The Revd Charlton Chinner with his wife and son William, pictured with livestock, 1917.

The choir in the early years of the twentieth century. Back row, left to right: -?-, Arthur Turner, George Turner, Josh Cartwright. Next row, left to right: -?-, Jack Turner, Harry Mathews, Revd Charlton Chinner, Percy Beddle, -?-, Harry Turner, John Yates (church warden). Seated far right on the third row is F.W. Hart (organist, choirmaster and schoolmaster).

School group outside Swindon School, 1900s. The schoolmaster is F.W. Hart, reputedly 'a terror with the cane'. The school was built in 1864 on a site close to the church and was enlarged in 1893. It moved to new premises in Wombourne Road in 1968 and a photographic studio now occupies the old building.

Pupils at Swindon School, 1935. Second row from front, second from right is Jimmy Turner. Third row from front, third from left is Gertie Turner, fourth from left is Joan Baines. Fourth row from front, fourth from left is Bessie Bache, fifth from left is Violet Clinton, fourth from right is Betty Williams. Fifth row from front, left to right: Nellie Turner, Joyce Davies, -?-, Elsie Bache, -?-, -?-, -?-, ? Watkiss, Kath Holford, Pat Blackham, Nancy Lamb, Florrie Turner, -?-, -?-, -?-, -?-, Muriel Hall, -?-. Back row, first from left is Norman Colwell, second from left is ? Collins.

Pupils at Swindon School, *c.* 1945. Mrs Porter (headteacher) is on the left, and Miss Fellows is the teacher on the right. Children attended the school from the villages of Swindon, Smestow, Wombourne and Himley. When they left, pupils went on either to Penzer Street School, Kingswinford, or to Manor Road School, Wolverhampton. Front row, left to right: Michael Hudson, -?-, Geoffrey Clinton, Peter Brough, Michael Harvey, -?-, Lawrence Sneyd, -?-, -?-, Brian Williams. Next row, left to right: Margaret Lampett, -?-, -?-, -?-, -?-, -?-, Shirley Noke, Jane Barnett, Peggy Postins, ? Sneyd, Frances Linney, Madeline Baker, Heather Watson, Pat Hall, June Cole. Third row, left to right: Wendy Greig, Audrey Grass, Sandra Barnett, Christine Bains, Pat Sneyd, Josie Collier, Thelma Davies, Kathleen Reynolds, Peggy Beddall, Edith Rowley, Valerie Bains, Janet Reynolds, Jean Reynolds, Carol Bache. Fourth row, left to right: -?-, -?-, Geoff Davies, -?-, -?-, Harry Collins, Ronnie Evans, Maurice Grass, Derek Cartwright, Howard Wenlock, -?-, George Piper, -?-. Back row, left to right: Michael Evans, Raymond Hall, -?-, Bobby Edwards, -?-, -?-, Dennis Collins, Derek Postins, -?-, Brian Piper, -?-, ? Lindley, -?-.

The oldest known view of Swindon ironworks, *c.* 1900. The photograph was found in the works. The history of ironworking in Swindon dates back to at least 1620. The first forge on this site was converted from a corn mill by Thomas Foley in 1647. In 1834 it was owned by George and Edward Thorneycroft of Wolverhampton and produced bar iron and wire rods. In 1866 it was leased to E.P. and W. Baldwin who were the owners by 1899. In 1873 the works consisted of twelve puddling furnaces and two mills, and produced sheet iron.

View from Hinksford Lane, 1950s. This shows how Baldwins' dominated the village at this time. In 1945 the firm became Richard Thomas and Baldwin Ltd and the main product was rolled silicon sheets for the electrical engineering industry. After nationalization the works were known as British Steel Corporation, Swindon Works.

The ironworks alongside the canal between Swindon Bridge and the Marsh Locks. The canal was of great importance for delivering materials and sending out products. The tow-path was originally on the opposite bank and was moved in 1915 so that the horses did not have to thread their way through the working men.

The works and canal, 1960s. The old bridge was replaced in 1975 and the chimney stack was built in the early 1940s.

The bar bank, 1950s. Iron bars are being offloaded to go to the hot rolling mill. The bars arrived each day from Stourbridge basin at 9 a.m. The crane driver is Bill Robinson. In later years the bars were delivered by lorry.

The rolling mill, 1950s. The sheet passed through the roller to be grabbed by the two 'catchers' who fed it through again. This process was repeated, and as the sheet got longer it was doubled up and put through again until the required gauge was achieved.

Steelmen, *c.* 1897. Tom Jones, the works foreman, is sitting front right, and his youngest son, Will, is the boy on the left sitting cross-legged.

Some of the last workers at BSC Swindon, 1975. Left to right: Mr Singh, Geoff Williams, Dave Turner, Mr Singh, Jim Bache, Alf Robinson, Geoff Bullock, Don Evans, Sid Kimberley.

The installation of Galloways steam rolling mill engine at Baldwins' works, shortly before the First World War. The man to the left of the nameboard is Tom Jones, the works foreman. Most of the other men were presumably from Galloways.

The Swindon works offices, 1960s. When the works closed in 1976, everything was demolished except for the canteen which was taken over by the parish council. It was reopened in 1981 as a community centre for the village.

The works house with the foreman, Tom Jones, and his daughter, Kate, and son, William, in the garden, *c*. 1903. The works are behind. Tom lived rent-free and received free coal all the time he lived in Swindon. He never really retired, becoming the time-keeper after his official retirement. At the age of 81 he came home from the early shift, sat down in his chair and died.

BBC commentators cruise past the works while making a radio programme in the early 1950s on canals in the Midlands. The commentators include Audrey Russell, Wynford Vaughan Thomas and Godfrey Baseley. The party stopped at the works to sign autographs.

Mr George Reynolds auctioning produce after the Flower and Vegetable Show held on the Manor House Farm meadow, 1940s.

Ice cream man, Vic Milano, selling ices. Left to right: Vic, Ernest Williams, Jack Young, George Billingsley and Joe Lampitt outside the Green Man, 1929.

Himley Village, *c.* 1947. This view is towards the Wolverhampton to Kidderminster Road. The scene has not changed very much over the years, and is now peaceful again since the completion of the bypass.

Himley Village, *c.* 1947. The same stretch of road from the opposite direction.

Himley Hall. The hall was built by the Earl of Dudley, *c.* 1740. The Dudleys were lords of the manors of Himley, Wombourne, Swindon, Dudley, Sedgley, Kingswinford and Rowley Regis. They were involved in mining and ironworking to exploit the minerals below their land. In 1845, William, Lord Ward and later the 1st Earl of Dudley, purchased Witley Court near Stourport. This became the family seat after a rival company developed an ironworks uncomfortably close to Himley. Himley Hall and Park were sold in 1947 and purchased by the National Coal Board for £45,000 to be used as their regional headquarters. The NCB in turn sold the property in 1967 to the councils of Dudley and Wolverhampton. The grounds are now a country park. The future of the hall has been uncertain, but current plans are to use it as a glass museum.

The original entrance gates and lodge to Himley Hall. The entrance is now for pedestrians only.

St Michael's Parish Church, Himley. The church was built in 1764 and incorporated pan-
elling and a rood screen from the hall's private chapel. In 1894 the church was refurbished
and the lych gate was added to mark Queen Victoria's Diamond Jubilee. A new porch and
vestry were added in the late 1980s. The only part of the grounds of Himley Hall that still
belongs to the Dudleys is the Garden of Memory, near to the church, where several members of the family are buried.

Himley House, former home of the Grazebrook family and now the Himley House Hotel.
Owen Grazebrook, the last owner, was a Worcestershire JP.

The wishing well, Himley Woods. The well was a tourist attraction but looked little like the modern idea of a wishing well. The lady with her pail appears to be collecting water for more mundane purposes.

The Glynne Arms, better known locally as 'The Crooked House', stands on the border of Himley and Gornal. The reason for the nickname is obvious and is due to mining subsidence. The plant hanging in the doorway gives a good idea just how out of true the building is.

The Glynne Arms before the First World War, looking somewhat different from today with its large car park and wooden tables. However the pub is still reached by a narrow lane and the atmosphere remains rural. The original name relates to a local landowning family.

The interior of The Crooked House looks even more bizarre than its exterior and the bottles and glasses appear to defy gravity. The number of photographs dating from the early years of the century demonstrate that it has been a local curiosity and object of tourism for many years.

Another interior of The Crooked House. Ball bearings are given to patrons today so that they can watch them apparently roll uphill!

The entrance to the present Baggeridge Country Park near the beginning of the twentieth century. The scene is still identifiable, although the large avenue of trees has disappeared.

A cottage in Baggeridge Woods. Many old postcards and views show that this area, parts of which are now in Baggeridge Country Park, has long been an attraction for daytrippers from the nearby Black Country. Photographs of the woods from before the Second World War show magnificent trees, many of which were felled to fuel the war effort. The area of woodland is now considerably smaller.

Baggeridge Colliery commenced production in 1912 and was the last mine established to work the Black Country ten-yard-thick coal seam. The colliery was operated by the Baggeridge Colliery Company Limited. It leased the land from the Dudley Estate in return for royalty payment. The coal was sent to the Round Oak Steel Works and all over the Black Country on a specially extended branch railway line connected to the GWR at Gornal. Baggeridge Brick Works was established next to the colliery in 1936 and is still in operation.

Baggeridge Colliery from the air, showing Baggeridge Woods behind. The mine closed in 1968 and the buildings were dismantled. The spoil heaps, one of which can be seen here, were rounded off and grassed over. They now form a feature of the present country park which was officially opened by Princess Anne in 1983. The tradition of providing recreational facilities for the industrial Midlands is still maintained in this area today.

Acknowledgements

The authors wish to thank the staff of the Wolverhampton Archives and Local Studies Department for their help, and Liz Rees, the archivist, for permission to reproduce photographs; also the staff of Stafford Record Office and the County Archivist, Dudley Fowkes, for permission to use photographs. Special thanks to Fred Nickholds and Robert Taylor who have made such excellent prints, sometimes from very poor originals, and to Derek Mills for proof-reading.

Personal acknowledgements from the three authors are as follows:

Peter Leigh, Pattingham
Ron Bond • Lilian Bowen • Mrs Bull • Lol Burgess • David Burton • Joe and Nancy Caddick • Angus Dunphy • Jack French • Norman Harris George Lloyd • Mrs Martin • A. J. Parkes • Norah Parkes • Pattingham Civic and Local History Society • Roz Poulton • Tom Ray • Robert Taylor Barbara Titley • Edna and George Wheeler • Roland Williamson *Wolverhampton Chronicle* • Wolverhampton *Express and Star* Wolverhampton Library.

May Griffiths, Wombourne
Angus Dunphy • Dennis Granger • Shirley Harris • Gilbert Harthill Florence Johnson • Weyman Jones • Glenda Knights • Ann Smith Mary Mansell • Mary Mills • John and Carolyn Phillips • David Piper Margaret Sadler • Dorothy Wick • Ned Williams Wolverhampton *Express and Star* • Dora Wooldridge. Special thanks to John and Poppy Holloway and Frank Blackwell for help over the years with copying photographs, and to husband John Griffiths for his support, always.

Mary Mills, Trysull, Seisdon, Swindon, Himley and Baggeridge
Mrs Brown • Mrs Janet Clarke • Angus Dunphy • Mr Charles Evans Mr Dennis Granger • May Griffiths • Mrs Margery Knott Mr and Mrs Alf Robinson • John Salmon • Ray Vye • Ernest Williams Special thanks to Mr F. Sutton who ensured that Seisdon was properly represented.

Apologies must go to anyone who has unwittingly been omitted from the list of acknowledgements.